D1140951

NONSENSE

Nonsense CHRISTOPHER REID

faber and faber

First published in 2012
by Faber and Faber Ltd
Bloomsbury House
74–77 Great Russell Street
London WC1B 3DA

Typeset by CB editions, London
Printed in England by T. J. International Ltd, Padstow, Cornwall

A CIP record for this book
is available from the British Library

ISBN 978-0-571-28128-2

10 9 8 7 6 5 4 3 2 1

Contents

Acknowledgements

Part of 'Professor Winterthorn's Journey' was included in the anthology *In Memoriam*, edited by Kirsty Gunn (University of Dundee); all of 'The Suit of Mistress Quickly', in Craig Raine's magazine *Areté*. 'Airs and Ditties of No Man's Land' was written to be set to music by Colin Matthews, commissioned by the City of London Sinfonia and first performed, as *No Man's Land*, at the BBC Proms in 2011; it was also published as a pamphlet by Rack Press. 'A Bit of a Tune' was in *The King's Lynn Silver Folio: Poems for Tony Ellis*, edited by Michael Hulse; 'Espresso', in *Poetry Ireland*; a version of 'Flute and Piano', in the *Listener*; 'La Tartuga', in *La Tortue Poétique*, edited by Bernard Turle; 'Dr Demon' and 'Neddy and the Night Noises', in the *London Review of Books*; 'Chorus', in *Raising the Iron: Poems for the Palace Theatre, Watford*, edited by David Harsent; 'A Pub Band', in *Wild Reckoning: An Anthology Provoked by Rachel Carson's 'Silent Spring'*, edited by John Burnside and Maurice Riordan; and 'Rabbits and Concrete', on a poster issued by the Poetry Trust. 'Solar System' and 'Raga' formed part of 10 + 2, with drypoints by Bryan Illsley (Paupers Publications). A number of the poems in 'A Salute to the Moonlight' were distributed in a small edition as *A Salute to the Moonlight* (Own Desk). I am grateful to all who have commissioned or published my work.

PROFESSOR WINTERTHORN'S JOURNEY

to Ben Sonnenberg

On a whim, Professor Winterthorn –
sixty years old, recently widowed –
resolves to attend. He'll fly in the morning.

His conference-roving days are waning,
but, while he's not been asked to speak
at this one, it's on a theme close to his heart:

Nonsense and the Pursuit of Futility
as Strategies of Modernist, Postmodernist
and Postpostmodernist Literature and Art.

Just in case, he has a paper almost written
that he can tuck into his hand-luggage
and tinker with on the plane.

(But he won't.)

Besides, what is there to keep him in London,
nobody at home, his friends dispersed
to the Baltic, the Peloponnese, the Mediterranean?

He'll outstrip them! With satisfaction,
he buys online, immaterial tickets,
fleet fingers performing their keyboard tap dance:

laptop dancers!

Check details, whirr of print-out – and it's done.
Good. He'll soon be in a distant city
which he's never visited and knows nothing about.

That's the point.

Could even be fun.

⌒

Now pack my bag:
not such an easy task.
Pondering and dithering,
deciding and undeciding,
he veers between wardrobe and suitcase.

Eight days away,
so a French week's worth
of shirts, jerseys, underthings
must somehow be flung
harmoniously together.

But how can he know beforehand
what he'll want to wear?
How both guess the weather
and avoid excruciating
colour clashes?

What did he do in the past?
Oh yes, he had a wife,
who was wise in such matters,
directing, advising, cajoling, dissuading him
in his difficult choices.

Tonight he must work it out for himself.
But the sock drawer is a bear-garden
of competitive voices;
none of his jerseys
wants to join in –

it's not so easy.

    ~

There's a wallet of photos
of his wife and himself, and his wife alone,
that he must take too.

Half a dozen snaps:
such flimsy documents
to bear the weight of a lost life.

Most precious and painful, perhaps,
is this one showing her
days before the final op:

gaunt, anguished, smiling, being brave.

About to slip them
into the heaped skip of his suitcase,
he blenches when it strikes him:

too much like a mass grave.

～

So they can go into his shoulder-bag tomorrow
along with a wodge of as-yet-untranslated currency,
passport, flight details, insurance documents, what not,
plus reading matter he can only decide at the last minute:

some big figure's neglected Collected Poems, possibly,
or austere classic that's been giving his conscience a bad
    time:
Broch, Gombrowicz, Robbe-Grillet, Bernhard – something
bracingly foreign, difficult and ugly –

But that's for tomorrow. Right now it's bedtime.

～

Not so much sleep as a buffeting,
a duffing-over, by brutal dreams.

Obscurely vengeful, they pounce on him
and carry out a questionless interrogation.

One after another, they arrive at his bed,
pop some idiot plotline in his head

and command him to follow it.

Which he does, like the accused in a trial by ordeal,
or contestant in a frenzied TV challenge show.

He awakes exhausted, sweaty, confused.
If not found guilty, he has at least been humiliated

and there is no appeal.

～

Through bath and breakfast –
burnt toast, black coffee –
Winterthorn worries away
at the hidden significance
of these scrambled narratives.

Of course he is aware
that a dream is not a text,
and poorly remembered
this batch in particular
must be deemed corrupt.

But he remains vexed
that he cannot decode them.
What is most tormenting
is that, while Clarissa
failed to appear personally,

she must be behind them.

So what was she trying to say?

Head full of this worry
and general pre-flight
flap and flurry,
he cannot stop to choose a book.
No problem: the airport rack

will yield some nice, fat, sedative paperback.

⁓

Skids on, so praise
to the invention of the wheel,
and praise to our suitcase
manufacturers'
belated discovery
and application of it!

From locked front door
to waiting taxi
it's an easy trundle.
Bumps and skips
against uneven paving-stones
add to the dash.

Ducking down and into
the cab's ample interior,
he clocks the generic
deodorised odour,
squirt of morning freshness,
then chunks the door shut.

Glassed-in, upholstered
and rapid solitude
for this stage of the journey
is what he wants.
He snuggles into the corner
diagonal to the cabby.

Not sure he likes
the back of that head:
scalp too intimately shaved
and dirtily dotted
with stubborn new growth –
but he needn't look closely.

And once on the road,
at least the fellow's not gabby
in that old Ealing Comedy
geezer style
of abhorrent opinion
and chummy oath.

Solitude and speed:
mile by mile,
London unravels
from stucco to stock brick,
leafed suburb to motorway.
Reverie of travel.

Till eventually straggles
and clusters of unreadable
airport buildings,
blank sheds, curved rampways,
gather him back
to himself and his purpose.

They've arrived.

That was quick.

～

Beyond the perpetually chomping glass doors
is where the process begins in earnest:
the rendering-down of the human unit
to what the system can digest and eject

thousands of miles away.

Winterthorn, from whom you might expect
resistance, has learned from decades of flying
all the arts of complying, and will obey,
scarcely feeling – or not showing he feels –

the assault on his inner self.

Check-in is slow but goes without a hitch;
he presents passport photo – tiny, yes, but me! –
joins the abattoir shuffle towards baggage inspection
and body frisk; and at last is admitted

to the great, luminous cavern of Duty Free.

~

The dread realm of waiting,
where for almost two hours
the traveller must submit
to the twin powers
of commerce and tedium.

Where time is a trickster
and the tantalising concessions
of the flight indicator board,
its sly twitch and shift,
are not to be believed.

Winterthorn would like to stretch
the exchange of his sterling
for improbable new notes
to an elaborate and lengthy negotiation,
but the girl is too brisk.

Purchase of a Speyside malt
takes no time at all;
ditto, detective novel.
So he joins the longest and slowest
queue he can find

at a coffee stall.

～

A vast cup of latte
and a dough-grenade muffin,
which he begins to dismantle.

Pleasant, the picking-apart
of crumb-and-berry clusters,
pinched to make edible pellets.

Chewing slowly is an art
revealed only after long study
to the most enlightened masters.

But he'll apply himself now:
a lone Zen pilgrim
camped and meditating by a muddy

lake of tepid latte.

～

Thus he sets himself apart
from the carnival
of suspended life
that continues around him,
in order to dwell
on the deeper absence
within himself:

the wife who is not there.

Absence within absence.
Parenthesis
within parenthesis
within parenthesis.
And at the heart:
nothing. Empty brackets.
A drear vacuum

that howls like hell.

⁓

Flight announced, he takes the long,
peristaltic trek to the departure gate.
A briefer and more concentrated wait.
He wonders which of the wondering strangers
he'll be sitting next to.

On board, oozy music and shallow smiles
from the cabin staff. He's near the back.
Is that good? Or dangerous?
Bag and bottle are put away up top.
He assumes his seat, new novel on lap.

Its weight is comforting.

(Not that he'll read it.)

His travelling companions on either side
are gratifyingly unintrusive.
Seats aren't wide, but they settle down
without territorial elbow-play
or shoulder-assertion.

All in this together.

Enjoy the ride!

⁓

Faith, hope
and aerodynamics
ensure safe take-off.

Even so, he misses
a fourth force:
light squeeze of linked hands.

Missing it, though,
means remembering it,
means feeling it – almost.

A ghost of familiar
pressure registers
against his left palm.

Then fades.

The plane continues
its steep, loud,
laborious ascent.

They enter cloud.

Be calm, be calm.

⁓

Professor A. J. Winterthorn
does not believe in God.
Even as a reasoning,
picturing and figuring child,
little Anthony found it too odd
that an old man living on a cloud –
broad and sun-paved like this one, perhaps –
should be looking down and watching
everything he did,
and everything everyone else did,
and deciding if it was good.

How could He have enough eyes?

Now hurtling through God-void skies
in a people-packed metal pod,
he doesn't exactly regret
the implausible, bearded, judging,
hymned-at, upper-case deity,
nor indeed the array of more modest
gods and goddesses
others might put there instead,
but he would like something better
to worship than the absurd.
As he's begun to say in the paper

that's stowed overhead.

～

Not writing, not reading,
he waits for the jolted and tinkling arrival
of the drinks trolley.
By stages, it reaches him down the narrow aisle.

A double dose of Scotch
from twin toy bottles
emptied over ice in a plastic tumbler
should do the trick. It does.

First lifting of that friendly, nuzzling fragrance
towards his nose
begins the treatment;
first, astringent sip continues it.

The plan is to spend
as much of the trip as he can asleep –
he's good at catching naps
in unpromising and uncomfortable places.

This works better than expected.

The nap that catches him
is more like a trance, or fugue:
a state of elation and detachment that permits
awareness of all around him, while he stays

aloof, invulnerable, virtually absent.

Flight within flight!
A higher plane of reality!
If anybody looked in his face now,
they might think he was mad.

Eyes wide, stark upright,
without lowering the back of his seat
or changing his posture,
he's away. But misses nothing.

Lunch comes, on trays
that buzz close to his head
but do not land on his little table-shelf.
Lit daylight turns to artificial dusk.

Others have ears clamped to music,
or eyes to movies –
a scattered and staggered multiplication of stories –
on tiny, private screens.

In his hypersensitive daze,
he can watch and follow every one
simultaneously
through gaps between head-rests:

dialogue, trite or witty,
easily, pentecostally lip-read;
intimate body language and cartoon violence
all the more immediate

in their distance and silence.

Another meal.

Then general slumber.

The seat in front of him lunges at him
but doesn't quite touch.
There are plastic clatterings at his back.
Twice, he gets up for his neighbour.

But nothing disturbs
the ecstatic repose
of his somehow anaesthetised
and surgically extracted self.

At length, however, he and his body
enter a sleep
that is real and deep.
When morning light shocks him awake,

he feels resurrected.

~

The sky is cloudless, blameless.
Brown mountains below,
or are they hills?
Much of a muchness.
Same old sameness.

Then flatter stuff,
with hints and sketches
of habitation.
Then suburban muddle's
fuzzy edges.

Then, loveliest of sights,
blue blaze of sea,
against which the infant
human settlement
trustingly cuddles.

That's the airport
tucked in down there:
journey's end,
if we hit it right.
Out over the bay now:

tilt, turn, aim straight, descend.

        ∿

From bump of landing to taxi queue,
it's a breeze, a wave-through.

He is standing in different daylight.
There are different colours. Different voices.

Different trees.

        ∿

Different taxis. This one, low-slung, lime-green,
looks at a glance as trustworthy as any.
Its driver, too, is promisingly dour.

Winterthorn takes it, names his hotel,
and off they go, slouching and swaying boatlike
into the flow and abrupt non-flow

of freeway traffic.

Though progress is spasmodic –
to use a word he would normally scold
his students for using, but now seems exactly right –

he is content to scan and make wrong guesses about
the passing scene: the special delight
of any new city, as he has learned from a hundred

ill-prepared arrivals.

Indeed, it has given him the theme of his book
The Pleasures of Misreading: one of his many
incomplete, or unbegun, theoretical projects.

Buildings, billboards, vehicles, landscaping,
roadside bric-a-brac, the whole topographic
razzmatazz, submit to his musings:

there to be plundered.

￼

But the closer they get
to the heart of the city,
there's something, there's something – what?
peaceable? pretty? –

about the arrangements,
about the appointments,
that denies Winterthorn
his habitual, witty,

dissociative, internal commentary.

Here are banks and office blocks.
So they're bang in the middle,
and yet there's an air
of he won't go so far

as to use the word idyll,

but –

~

But the hotel where he has booked,
the Intercosmopolitan,
is the usual bland asylum.

In a lobby sluiced with muzak,
he presents himself for welcome
and electronic certification.

The lift, a cage of mirrors,
takes him and his multiple reflections
up to the eighth floor.

Room 808. He dunks
his key-card, shoulders open the door,
and there's his new home.

Superfluous square metres of bed.
Giant TV. A bathroom
that roars when you switch the light on.

Nothing, of course, to tell you
who has stayed here before,
or who will in the future,

or who is doing so now.

⌒

Time to assert himself,
to make his presence felt.
There's a sheet of telephone numbers
folded in his jacket pocket.
Contacts is the name of the game.

Tony Winterthorn here –
That's right, right on your doorstep.
Wondered if I could drop by
on this nonsense conference of yours.
Purely as a spectator.

Ba-boom, he's in! As ever,
the international freemasonry
works a treat, reminding him
how clever it is to be clever.
Now to unpack, step out

and grab a bite to eat.

⌒

He unpacks his suitcase
as he might unpack a novel,
to demonstrate to the author
what he or she really meant:
chaos of contents
transmuted to ideal order,
with separate drawers for each theme,
and wardrobe hangers

clarifying the plot.

In similar spirit, he spills out
the farrago of his shoulder-bag,
analysing and arranging it
on the dressing-table/desk.
That's more like it!
Only suddenly it strikes him
like a ghostly blow to the midriff:
the photographs –

He completely forgot –

~

He sits on the end of the bed, winded, sickened.
How could he have allowed it to happen?

Clear as day, he can see the SnipSnaps wallet
waiting next to his desk-lamp, half a world away.

A crime, a betrayal, has been committed
and plainly his memory is the culprit,

but it must have been aided and abetted.

So he'll sit there on the bed and be self-interrogated
for as long as it takes. Till he coughs up the why and the
    wherefore.

Till his stupid resistance breaks.

~

From a long, eventless sleep, he wakes
to evening. City-lit dusk
seeps through wall-wide window-blinds.

Unabsolved by dreams, he finds
that, while his remorse about the photos
is still acute, so is his hunger.

Therefore he must get out and eat.
Too hurried to wash or shave,
he puts on his heaviest jumper to smother

a two-day traveller's musk.

Out in the street, with a simplified
hotel map – the kind he prefers – to guide him,
he sets off in any direction.

Getting lost is a favourite occupation,
grist to the iBook, but right now
he hasn't time for that.

Nor for systematic crowd-dissection.
His one purpose is to take, to brave,
the first restaurant he comes to.

Chinese? That will do.

Delighted by the row
of hanging orange ducks –
Chinese mistranslation
of duck à l'orange! –
he orders one as a starter.

Squid in chilli sauce to follow.
Lashings and lashings of MSG!
And to wash the feast down,
a rotund pot
of scented tea –

refill later.

The chair on the other side
of the tiny table
remains unoccupied.
Photoless, he tries to see
Clarissa sitting there,

but is unable.

～

Twelve stories high,
twelve rooms per floor,
the hotel at night
is a hive of dreams.

Room by room,
cell by cell,
dreamwork proceeds
on private themes.

Don't be misled
by grunt and zizz:
the purpose is
a healing sweetness.

Prone on his bed,
Winterthorn,
a worker bee,
is employed as well

at this mighty, snoozing industry.

～

He sleeps and sleeps
beyond hotel breakfast hours.
No problem: a whole day
of dolce far niente
lies ahead
and, from what he can spy
of weather in the gaps
between odd-shaped office blocks,
it's going to be a fine one.

Leisurely, he shaves and showers,
enjoying the plenty
of pounding hot water
longer than he needs to,
then two towels
to get extravagantly dry.
After which, he dallies over
the ideal combination
of shirt, socks and tie.

Funny money
fattening his wallet,
he steps out on to the town
with a carefree air.
The day crowd differs from the night one:
more driven, more milling and blending,
more of a contrast
to the skitter and ricochet
of his own present mood.

For elevenses breakfast,
as he decides to call it,
he chooses a busy café
and a windowside chair
with a view of several streets.

A waitress brings coffee
and a peachy pastry.
As he eats, he opens a notebook
and begins to stare.

Who says it's rude?

⁓

He has another essay on the go –
Alphabet Soup: Typography of the Crowd –
about the human unit's search for meaning
within the random urban group,
and the tragi-comic predicament whereby
it cannot read the shifting sentences
of which it forms an involuntary part.

Back home, he's made a small but promising start,
and the adjacent, ample window-view should yield
material enough – nothing to beat
work in the field! Somehow, though,
he cannot engage,
and by the end of the morning all he's written
is two words at the top of the page:

Bugger Barthes.

⁓

Slightly portly, pastry-fed Professor Winterthorn
leaves the café at 12:45.

Where cars have stopped at a crossing, he crosses,
encouraged by a fit of the jitters from the little green man.

He reaches a street of department stores and boutiques:
no city-slicing avenue, this, nor grandiose boulevard,

though his hotel map insists it's the main drag.
More like the centre of a British provincial town.

He strolls, halting at windows, which present
their merchandise as the poems in a little mag

present their meaning: so eager to be liked,
they scarcely hold his attention.

To the left, an enticingly featureless one-way street
distracts him, and he toddles down that;

then down another, more off-beat.
Map in pocket, he now commits himself

to a wholly intuitive, zigzag course that, too soon,
brings him back to his hotel.

Go up? Might as well.

～

Phone winking at him. He plays the message. Plays it again.
Astrid, his one-time student! How did she fetch up here?
Clever, wilful, garish, infuriating Astrid.
It's an office number, so he dares to return the call.

Her office voice. Then she laughs, more recognisable.
Nothing's a secret, she says, in this tiny parish.
If you scratch your bum, next day it's front-page news.
So of course I heard in ten minutes. Thrilled you've come.

Turns out she's married: both in the department.
His loss? She knows, is breezily condoling,
which, almost two years on, still irks him.
Want of the proper, sombre tone.

But what's the point of nattering on the phone,
when they can meet? This evening? Yes, why not?
There's a tolerable spot just down the street.
Good. For a quick one, as she'll have to dash home.

Kiddies.

Of course.

Fine.

Understood.

～

To kill the afternoon,
he has his airport novel:
a 400-page-long
Scandinavian tale
of murder and detection,
set in the dark
and blizzardy far north.

For several chapters,
the murder itself –
wholesale family butchery –
is starkly recounted.
Now enter our detective:
loner, grouch and drinker
on the heroic scale.

Also, he writes poems.
From first appearance, it's plain
he's destined to fail,
and the author seems to take
a peculiar, teasing delight
in showing how he gets
every clue wrong.

Winterthorn is hooked.
Outside, it's sunny and bright,
but in his eighth-floor room
he lapses contentedly
into northern gloom.
Hours pass,
he's half-way through –

and suddenly it's night.

~

He's very late. Either she's been
and impatiently gone, or she's even later.
The latter.

Sorry, I went straight home to the kids.
Martin's with them now. He wants to polish the paper
he's giving tomorrow morning.

On his own translation of Finnegans Wake
into Irish, some of the difficulties.
Is it now? Thanks for the warning.

(This not said aloud.)

It's a cosy bar. They select a discreet banquette.
The piped music is bebop: lean, with pacy percussion,
spiked by a nice, sour trumpet.

They talk small talk: the who, the what, the when.
She's grown more beautiful, he thinks,
recalling a word that came to him earlier:

garish!

No longer right. Just lavishly blossoming.

Martin sounds a class-A prick. What is it with men
like him – humourless, pushy, egocentric –
that they snap up the brightest girls?

He tries to peer between the words.
Is she sending out a sign
that she's already tired of that dry stick?

By now, they've had a couple of drinks.
Suppose he moved in closer, put a hand on her knee?
Well, come on, he's no longer married,

no longer her doctoral supervisor.

But she's thirty years younger, and, on consideration,
non-interference seems wiser.
Instead, he gets up to fetch another round.

On his return, there's more chit-chat. Then she asks
what he's been working on.
Translating Nabokov back into Russian.

She nods, as if at something profound.

    ∿

That night, Clarissa
visits him in a dream,
but not in disguise,
as she often does;
she's just herself
thirty years younger.

Oddly, she's playing a cello –
melodious grumble and buzz –
until she gets stuck
on a particular phrase,

which she has to attack with her bow
again and again.

The mellow rumble
turns to a baby's howl,
fractious, unappeasable;
but still she plays,
or tries to pacify,
the empty-bellied instrument

whose voice is hunger.

~

Wind has got up in the night
and is still roaming the streets.
As he waits, Professor Winterthorn
watches it whipping and flapping
the scarves and coat-hems
of scurrying office workers,
so carefully carrying
their lidded paper cups of coffee,
chalices of cherished warmth,
up concrete steps
and into the lobbies
of lofty business palaces.

For a moment, he feels
a pang – of what? purpose-envy?
But as soon as his taxi draws up,
his own sense of purpose
revives. He's off:
to the brain fair, the jawfest,
the three-ring circus of argumentation
for which decades in a swivel chair
in a campus office,

pulling books to pieces
for the entertainment of students,
have singularly equipped him.

The University huddles
at the top of a hill.
As the taxi arrives,
he surveys the gallimaufry
of adapted domestic buildings
and award-winning architects' folly.
And that must be the conference hall,
already attracting
its swarm of chattering academics,
the very sight of whom –
such are today's mood swings –
has him turning

mildly melancholy.

~

Registration.
Bestowal of badges.
Because he's a late-comer,
Winterthorn's is handwritten –
and he likes that greatly.

In a drawer back home,
he keeps a collection
of his own name written
in different hands.
Hundreds of specimens.

They're his signatures, only
done by other people:
certification

of his fissile, multiple
public identity.

He must work that up some day.

Meanwhile, nothing more sweetly lonely
than a name on a lapel
in a room full of strangers,
who can only tell
who you are

by bending forward and squinting.

He likes that as well.

∿

But then he's recognised
by somebody he recognises:
Emiliana Vaporelli!

Excellent.
She waves and grimaces a greeting.
He nods back his.

And there's beautiful Astrid,
with what must be her husband:
exactly as imagined.

And there's little Hans Nagelman.
And there's Brannegan Wong,
today's keynote speaker.

Of course, he's already speaking:
rousing his commando force
of research students and acolytes,

who couldn't look meeker.

∿

Brannegan Wong
goes on too long.
Brannegan Wong
sings the same old song.

Brannegan Wong
with his luminous dong
and his numinous pong
comes on too strong.

But more than that
Brannegan Wong
of the voluminous
ongbongpong

is wrong.

~

What did you make of that?
he asks Hans Nagelman.

They are outside in the high wind.
Hans is smoking.

He takes a puff.
Nonsense, he replies –

appropriately enough.

No, no, I'm not joking.

~

Winterthorn inspects
the almost too-rich programme.
Just this afternoon,
there's a plethora of papers
on such topics as Dada

and the Armageddon of Sex;
Satie versus Music;
Was Beckett the First Goon?;
Silence in Céline and Celan –
How to choose between them?

Then what to choose next?
He looks up past the roofline,
where the wind is still busy
tousling the tops of trees.
That's when it strikes him:
Do as you please!
Dream up your own topic:
The Absence of Winterthorn
from Too Much Talk!
It's perfect, blustery,
soul-purging weather.

He'll take a long walk.

~

Escaping the campus, he plunges back down into town.
The wind is his walking companion. As good as a dog.
One moment, it leaps its great weight at him,
too friendly, almost unbalancing;
the next, it's away, wholly absorbed in wind business,
chasing street litter, worrying hedges,
poking its nose into cottagy front gardens,
then back at some street corner, to deliver
another rough shove. Down, boy! Down!

Its exuberant and inventive play
makes him feel more alive, more alert,
more in and of the world.
It also makes him feel, acutely, the old hurt

of his wife not being there with him,
to enhance his enjoyment by enjoying the same things.
So it could be the wind, or it could be this reflection, that
   brings
moisture to his eyes. No falling tears. Just a mist
that faintly prickles and blears.

Down into town: into the pretty city,
which seems to like to have the wind running through it.
Winterthorn pursues his unsystematic investigations
of the day before. That way, he finds the Parliament
   Buildings,
postmodernist, lopsided; the Cathedral, a big wooden box
with a squat bell-tower; the miniature Opera House.
And all of a sudden, he's at the harbourfront:
an arena of choppy waters circled by quays and jetties,
where a man can stand alone in the spray, in its lashing
   sidelong shower,

and bear the brunt.

⁓

After a hot bath, several times topped up,
he gets into bed with his detective novel,
malt in a toothbrush tumbler on his bedside table,
pillows at his back, one lamp reading over his shoulder:

all nice and snug.

Our detective hero has met a beautiful woman
and his heart is beginning to thaw, drip by icicle drip:
a process so reluctant, a less earnest reader might skip
a chapter or two, or doze as if through a half-heard
   sermon.

But Winterthorn continues at a deliberate trudge,
dwelling on each sentence almost as if he were trying
to slow the already sluggish action down, defying
such pull as there is towards a decisive edge.

He's eighty pages/three inches of whisky on,
when, in the real world, the phone makes its violent noise.
At the second summons, Winterthorn obeys.
It's Emiliana. What do you mean? Of course, I'm alone.

I'm downstairs, in the detestable bar. Please rescue me.

Give me ten minutes. No, fifteen.

     ~

Quick sticks. But not too quick.
Italian, she demands both care and flair.
Best jacket and pressed trousers on,
he combs his hair, then adds a few
disarraying finger flicks.

Debonair!

Whisky breath brushed and gargled away,
toilet flushed, then flushed again,
he's ready. Not quite.
May need a coat. What sort of night?
He goes to the lowered blinds,

parts slats, peeps and finds –

     ~

It's well into evening, but the city is still at work.
Lights are on in the neatly-stacked, glass offices
that he can observe from his privileged window.

Fiat lux, and then some: revealing, like hundreds of TVs
tuned to different channels, all mid-episode,
so many stories he cannot hope to follow.

But let him concentrate on one, chosen at random.
Floor nine? Ten? Eleven! A corner room, with a view
perhaps better than his, though not right now being enjoyed.

Instead, its occupant, a woman, sits at a desk
corporately black and minimalist but bearing
the standard office clutter: computer, telephone, paperwork,

inscrutable handbag spill.

Enter, behind her, a man in shirtsleeves, who strides past.
From the nod he aims at the back of her head, he must be
addressing her, but she makes no evident response.

Exit the man, possibly annoyed. She stands up
and, in profile, locking her hands at her nape, stretches:
a slender, almost abstract, but wholly voluptuous shape.

You could read her mind, if you were God, or a novelist.

Or had the time, or the will.

　　　　～

The hotel's cocktail bar
is a den of lilac light
and simpering mood-music.
Trite! The most pejorative word
in Emiliana's lexicon.
I cannot stay here a moment longer.
Such banality! And the price
of a whisky sour, my dear,
which was anyhow almost all
melting ice!

Her recitative of indignation
sees them out and fifty metres
down the road, where she stops.
Now, you like Mexican?
Good. There's a most amusing place
in the next street. Take my arm.
He does: such is her power.
Linked, they arrive
at a den of sulphurous light
and hectoring carnival music,

where they choose a table and order margaritas.

⁓

I had to escape.
A whole hour of King Wong!
A bow-tie is a thing of joy forever.

Ha! Very clever.
But tell me how long
you've been waiting to say that.

She smiles archly.

He smiles coyly.

Oh, I've said it before.
A few times.
In the most discreet company, of course.

Feminine company?
With a very red fingernail
she chips at the frosting of salt on the rim of her glass.

Let it pass.

⁓

Because what's on his mind
is their two bodies lying,
spent but still entwined,
on a catafalque-like bed
in Budapest.

Himself searching his head
for words to explain,
when he got home,
the irrefutable scratches
now smarting on his back.

And the bedside phone
chirruping, unanswered.
Which in due course he learned
was Clarissa calling
to report the results

of her hospital test.

⌒

Less tangled web than foolish botch:
beginner's slack and gappy macramé!

How did it go: a free afternoon –
walk in woodland – scrape with a thornbush –?

Not just that he so ineptly lied
bothers him now; but that Clarissa,

with her keen intelligence,
disdained to examine such obvious twaddle:

preoccupied.

⌒

You seem preoccupied.
Rude of me. Sorry.
Don't be. I know
you're thinking of your wife.

How long since she died?

Almost two –

My dear, in terms of mourning,
nothing at all. The dead,
I have to tell you,
never efficiently go.

They keep returning.
My own Umberto
still pays the occasional call,
not always well-timed or welcome.

One more little something
he remembers he left behind
and he happened to be passing
and he hopes I don't mind –

But frequently I do,
if I'm busy or there's a visitor,
and I have to say, Shoo,
you ridiculous old man!

Go! Come back later!

~

No, not you,
she says to the waiter,
who has pulled alongside
with plates of the peppery
peasant stodge

that Winterthorn must somehow
pretend he enjoys.

Jeering trumpets
and hard-flogged drums
make their indefatigable noise;
the restaurant thrums:
aural camouflage,
behind which his thoughts
can pursue their private business.

Emiliana's experience
seems quite different from his.
Yes, the dead do return,
but never so casually
and never exactly as they were.
He couldn't imagine shooing
Clarissa away.

Even before the end,
through the last, grim
episode of her dying,
she appeared to him
to be gradually withdrawing
to some province of unreality:
banishment he was forbidden to share.

Or was she in the real world,
and he the outcast?
That's what it sometimes felt like;
feels like now,
as he glances across the table
at his dinner companion
attacking her chow –

whiffy, dough-swaddled, beige-grey sludge –

with all her pounce and poise.

⌒

And before? Before Budapest?
Stockholm, Toronto, Buenos Aires –
Seven steps is all it takes
to trace the series
back to where it began.

A dance of seven steps
with pauses, sometimes of years, between:
how international,
how lightsome and how notional
his infidelity had been!

Yet that's a living, breathing,
emphatically present
woman sitting and eating there.
And his wife was once more present than that:
till she began to disappear.

Or he did.

What happened?

⌒

As Emiliana talks shop,
academic tittle-tattle,
he has time to consider her beauty.
Is it anything more than a brittle
construct of style,
a paradox of art?

In her early fifties,
she is still a pretty
and precocious little schoolgirl,
with a bossy air that he reads
as a plea for affection,
and a wooingly wolfish smile.

And what her clothes, so smart,
so formidably à la mode,
in fact conceal –
Oh, for godsake, stop
this quibbling dissection,
listen to her properly

and finish your meal!

~

Which he doesn't. He can't. He pushes his plate aside,
while admiring the despatch with which Emiliana
has cleared hers. So! Appetite satisfied,
she toasts her own triumph with the dregs of her drink:

Down the hatch!

Her English, Winterthorn reflects, is not the least –
But there he goes again. Enough! Bestirring himself
back to the conversational context,
he's aware he's missed a few steps, but perhaps can bluff.

Yes? Sorry, it's this infernal music.
Who'd live in Mexico? Day of the Dead
every day of the year! Doesn't it make you sick?
What's that you said just now? I didn't quite hear –

I was asking why you've come so far to attend
an event at which you've not been invited to speak,
and from which you seem mainly determined to abscond.
Was it to meet an old friend? Or to play hide-and-seek?

Ah. Yes. Why. I don't really know.
Something to do with returning to life
after a sentence of exile? Feeling I was due
a holiday from grief? Something like that, I guess.

And of course I was hoping that you –

That you and I –

⁓

Antonio, please. Permit me to interrupt.
Naturally, I am overjoyed to see you here.
Capturing and clinching both his hands
with one of hers, she leans towards him,
as if to whisper, under the music,
an intimate suggestion
warmly into his eager ear.

But, she continues, what you are thinking
is out of the question.
It would be wrong. It's plain
from your abstracted manner
that you're not really with me now.
You're with your dead wife.
Haven't you fallen in love with her again?

Startling Emiliana!

Their two stares lock, unblinking.

⁓

The hotel lift ascends,
bearing not just himself,
but a platoon of diminishing Winterthorns
that on either side of him bends
away to invisibility.

He'd like to see both ends,
but can't, even by slyly
adjusting stance and eyeline.
For the few, sharply surging
seconds of the journey

he enjoys the game, the futility.

⁓

Back in 808, he pours
a knock-out nightcap
and zaps on television.
First up is motor racing:
cars like jet-powered lobsters
whine round a track,
flirting with collision.

Next, frenzied rock stars.
Then a grey man at a desk.
Then chattering cartoon characters
of some unidentifiable species.
Then a woman doing exercises
in tight but stretchy clothing.
Then golfers inspecting sky.

One minute has gone by.

One minute of total narrative incoherence.

Winterthorn decides
he needs a calmer pace.
Zapping off, he prepares
for bed with his new friend,
the Scandinavian detective,
whose adventures, he's sad to notice,
are coming an end.

One thing's for sure:
he's going to lose his girl.
Another: within the next few
pages he'll pour
a drink: a large one.
Winterthorn is ready
to present his own tumbler

for a sympathetic clink.

～

The detective, however, is less sympathetic,
less of a soulmate, than expected.

No companionable clinking. How could there be?
Winterthorn reflects, holding his plastic tumbler.

His reception is curt, if not downright rude:
You took your time, sir. Something to hide?

Before Winterthorn, who at once feels hurt,
can voice an objection, the fellow continues:

I must say, you've been uncommonly clever,
leading me a dance from the very first page.

The whole murder thing, the bloodbath in the barn,
has been a distraction, as I might have guessed.

Then to dangle that schoolteacher in front of my nose:
well, really, at my age, I should have known better.

Cherchez la femme, as the saying goes,
though, in this case, la femme turns out to be

outside the story, if you catch my drift.
As I believe you do, to judge from your expression.

Slow on the uptake, but I see it all now:
this hasn't just been some ordinary, gory

murder yarn, with clues and a fancy solution,
but one of those – what you call – postmodernist fables.

Right. Care to let me have your confession?

⁓

He wakes in sitting position, but slumped,
with a neck pain. His book is still open.
His tumbler has tumbled off the bed.

His top sheet displays an expansive
whisky stain, dampish, reeking.
Attempts to swab it away

merely spread it further.

One-man farce: the murderer
blunders about the stage, or cage,
of his guilt and panic. But why bother?

Let his disgrace be known!

The chambermaid will have seen worse.

⁓

The universal language of breakfast music,
Winterthorn writes in his notebook.
Aspirational pop.
Related to hymns and marches:
fills your heart with hope
then drums you out of the front door
at the double and off to work.

He reads what he has written.
Could be true, but does it get you anywhere?
Nope. So he crosses it out,
rips, or unzips, the page from its spiral binding,
squashes it up
into the tightest,
most spherical ball he can make

and drops it into his coffee cup.

⁓

By taxi to campus, under the sweetest sunlight.
Though that's a reason for staying out of doors,
he'll try to put in full attendance this morning.
Two items, at least, on the programme look worth
    listening to.

At nine-thirty, there's Astrid, his star student,
on Some Thanatological Themes in The Third Policeman;
and later, Hans Nagelman on Edward Lear:
a guaranteed fifty minutes of wisdom and learning.

(Other names serve more as a timely warning.)

The massed troops are being victualled with coffee and
    biscuits.
Inserting himself obliquely into the throng,

Winterthorn is quickly attuned to certain absences:
Emiliana? And the egregious Wong?

They couldn't be –

No, Wong must be half-way round the world already
and addressing some other conference, unlucky sods!
While Emiliana: well, what are the odds
she's nursing Mexican tummy back in her hotel?

Let's join the fray!

~

Astrid's paper
is dry and dutiful.
What happened
to all her beautiful,
wayward sparkle?
Did he himself
knock it out of her
all those years ago?

Could be so.

Poor, bibulous O'Brien's
macabre caper
is briskly reduced
by means of theory,
or intellectual
pseudo-science,
to a misbegotten tract.
How wrong! How dreary!

But then again,
maybe she's right.
Hasn't his own mind

been in flight
from full recognition
of the One Big Fact?
Perhaps her strictures
are aimed at him –

To know about death
but not to know it
imaginatively:
name me the poet
or novelist –
especially one
who is generally pissed –
who isn't guilty!

Name me the husband
of a dying woman
who doesn't feel
less than human
because he can't
share her experience,
because, for him,
death isn't real!

Thus Winterthorn
half-listens, half-muses,
while his one-time student
earnestly confuses
a Dublin boozer's
sports and fancies
with serious thoughts
on serious themes.

Or so, to him, increasingly it seems.

⁓

Question time. Chair
scans the room for hands.
Professor Winterthorn?

Why is mine in the air?

Puzzled hesitation.
Then Chair again:
Professor – ?

Yes, thank you.
Not so much a question
as a tangential remark.

Though first I'd like to say
how thought-provoking that was:
shedding both light and dark

in equal measures.

Whereof one cannot speak,
thereof one must make
the best possible joke.

That seems to me the human plight,
as Flann, or Myles, or plain old Brian
understood it.

Which puts us plodding commentators
on the spot,
does it not?

Condemned to explain the joke
to simple folk
who have got it already.

Thereby raising the suspicion
that we're the only ones
who haven't got it.

A worse hell,
a more extreme perdition,
than even our author conceived.

Have I said enough?

‿

Surprised by Astrid's
wounded, furious
and tear-edged glare,
he tries to send back
an appeasing signal:
Sweet, clever girl,
that's me, not you,
I was talking about there.

But he can't manage
the appropriate facial expression,
and anyway Chair
has taken the discussion
in another direction,
and she must go with it,
leaving him to rue
the unintended,

unundoable damage.

‿ ·

As the lecture hall empties, Winterthorn keeps his back-
   row seat.
He'd like to use the ten-minute break to examine his own
   state of mind –

and where better than an auditorium with no windows,
  steeply raked,
all eyes led sharply down to a whiteboard wiped blind?

Wife-loser, enemy-maker, sympathy-craving recluse,
he sits there fondling his burden of self-pity:
that most anti-magnetic of human emotions,
as he has begun to discover since arrival in this distant city.

And now to be pitying himself for the plight his self-pity
  has landed him in!
Help! There must be some way out of this trap, this
  syndrome,
or what would he have gained from venturing so far from
  home?
When the audience returns to hear Hans Nagelman

on Edward Lear, Our Contemporary, Winterthorn sits tight.

~

But not for long. As soon as Hans begins,
in his Viennese sing-song,

There was an Old Man on some rocks,
Who shut his wife up in a box,

there's a groan from the back row,
some scuffle and clatter,

Excuse me, please, I have to go,
acceleration and crescendo

of footsteps through an acoustic
that seems designed to magnify

any interruption,
anything untoward or awry,

and Winterthorn is last seen
shoving through the double doors,

which swing behind him – once, twice,
a third time –

with muffled force,
whereupon Nagelman completes

the absurd rhyme:
When she said, Let me out,

He exclaimed, Without doubt,
You will pass all your life –

portentous, Freudian pause –

in that box.

          ⁓

Down half-dark, unfamiliar stairs
and through a door he never came in by,
Winterthorn staggers like a drunk man
out into what must be
the student car park.

Clean, breathable air. Blue sky.
Sun on a concrete paddock of peaceable vehicles.
Students ambling to and fro
in that goofy, scruffy style of theirs
that gets less readable, less reasonable,

with the passage of the years.

Right now, though, it's exactly the thing
he wants, or needs, to see.
This campus is their kindergarten

and they are (car-driving) children:
unformed, future-friendly, free.

He stands and stares,
like a voyeur.
Or like a visionary.
Across the forty-year divide,
he feels, for once, provisionally,

on their side.

⁓

Enough, that is, to be bunking off
for the second day in a row.
Now, where to go?

I know: run away to sea.

At least, to see the sea.

His feet have memorised the map:
downhill – and there you are.
And it's not far.

Nothing in this place is far.

No wind, no dog, for company,
so he'll take his wife instead
and point out points of interest.

The idea lends his step a certain zest.

⁓

And here's the harbourfront,
where I fetched up yesterday
and, for some reason, stood
in the wind and spray

letting myself get drenched.
It was different weather then.
I must have thought
it would do me some good.

Love the light on the water now:
elastic, throbbing.
And look at those yachts out there,
catching what breeze they can.
And isn't that a four-man
skiff, or scull, or something,
heroically bobbing
through a sea that must be shoulder-height?

On a day, in a place, like this,
all activity,
even the yowling and prowling
of hungry gulls,
has the air of a dance:
an expression of delight in being.
You must know what I mean –
you, who did your dying

with such energy and bliss.

         ∾

When she doesn't reply –
of course, she can't, she's dead –
he's left to weigh for himself
the right/wrong
of what he's just said.

Activity as dance?
It seems to him, in this light,
it would be hard to call

her last, immobilised days
any kind of dance.

Yet he'd felt her floating away
like the belle of the ball,
rapt in the embrace
of a rival partner,
while he had had to look on:

jealous, impotent, shrivelling,

back to the wall.

~

Self-pity again:
that foolish trap
into which he seems to fall
with all the inevitability
and gravity – pun! –
of a slapstick comedian.

So that's him, is it?
The Buster Keaton of grief!
For a moment, he sees himself
stiffly toppling
off the end of the jetty
like an ornament off a shelf.

Splosh!

But no, come on,
it's too brilliant a day for that,
with the dazzle on the water
muscularly flexing
and the fighty flight
of gulls up above.

And that boat being rowed,
through a heavy wash,
closer to land.
Which he now can tell is manned
by women: four –
plus miniature cox

perched alertly at the stern.

⁓

What a surprise!
What a gift from the sea!
It's Aphrodite
multiplied by four.

(Or four and a half.)

Straining shoulder,
thigh and calf,
they pull in unison
towards the shore.

Such discipline:
to disguise the sweating,
hurting efforts
of a human team

in the lightness, fineness
and complexity
of a grasshopper –
wrong number of legs?

So? –

in the flash and dash of a dream!

⁓

Which passes.

~

Then it's such a beautiful day,
he's not quite sure what to do with it.

The sun's in the sky, where it should be,
free of clouds and beyond deconstruction.

The sea is the sea and no more:
unironically being itself.

And the world under his feet –
no-nonsense concrete at this point –

is simply and securely
a solid a man can stand on.

Or a woman, if she were here.

That's the puzzle he can't solve.

He catches sight of a bar
with benches and tables outside.

A nice, cold – an ice-cold – beer?

~

Alone on a broad bench,
with a tall glass of beer
for sparkling companionship.
Auprès de ma blonde –
the voice that does the singing
inside his head,
somewhere near the roots of his neck,
sings, with truer pitch
and in better-accented French

than he could muster –
Qu'il fait bon, fait bon, fait bon!

And that's the world
spread out before him:
the sea blinging
with an impenetrable lustre
under a sun both benevolent
and indifferent,
mountains beyond that watching
faint and aloof,
and the harbour itself
with its maritime industrialia
spick and span in fresh paint.

It must be lunchtime,
because here come the joggers,
jouncers and jogglers,
in all varieties of dress,
from charity-grunge and clown-baggy
to buttock-enhancingly tight,
to make their offering
of overflowing energy
to the supreme god of light.
The light gives them life
and they return it

in an ever-hopeful cycle.

Which puts him in mind of his wife.

~

When a life ends –
he's fumbling for the words –
where does, not the life,
but the life of the life go?

There can't be nothing to show.

There must be more than memory
and a rack of clothes
and some documents in a box.
Mustn't there?

Lives aren't like clocks,
that one day just stop
and can't be wound up
and need to be thrown away.

Are they?

Something as complex
as the galaxy
in which it exists
must have somewhere to go next.

All that religious stuff,
the blackmailing fallacy
of Heaven and Hell,
is plainly not good enough.

But what instead?
Do these pagans,
these lunchtime sun-votaries,
have the answer:

that winded plodder there,
cheek flushed
dark as a bruise,
that springy-thighed, pony-tailed prancer?

They give themselves to the light
unstintingly;
they don't refuse
the moment's imperatives.

By vital right,
they inhabit the present,
as I believe you did
and I have seldom, if ever, done.

O absent one!

～

He's not feeling maudlin, though.
On the contrary,
a world-suffusing good cheer
seems to have him in its grip,
as he dallies over his beer.

Sip. Long pause. Sip.

Time to get his troubles,
such as they are, in perspective,
and let the beer surrender its bubbles
from what it pretends
is an inexhaustible source.

Another pause, either reflective

or deliciously blank.

Sip.

～

Auprès de ma blonde,
the voice starts up again
its simple, mechanical song.

With the sunlight on his face
and his beer at hand,
Professor A. J. Winterthorn

stares into the mild, blue yonder.

⁓

And the yonder stares back –

Qu'il fait bon dormir.

THE SUIT OF MISTRESS QUICKLY

for Gwyneth Powell and Alan Leith

Somebody's not at home. Somebody's taken
an unscheduled holiday. Somebody's
not entirely with us

Rats, that's me!

Dudley's voice
has lost its normally studied languor:
prim now, prickly and whippish.

She's stung. She's sorry.
But where could she have been?
It feels an age

Quickly. Quickly, darling –

his camp form of address for her
mollifies, somewhat, the rebuke –

if you'd care to favour us with your presence,
your full presence –

light lash of nettle, just to remind her,
in the emphasis on full –

we'll try it again.
Top of the page.

⁓

Where could I have been?

A long way from this godforsaken church:
altar ripped out from the business end
organ-pipes too stout to shift from the other
but disconnected from their air supply and mute now

A long way, too, from Eastcheap,
Shakespeare's Asboland
of louts and larrikins and layabouts
where he set this charming scene.

        ~

Top of the page, boys and girls.

Which page, Dudley?

Sir Geoffrey, of course, big bristled baby
broadcasting his gargantuan need
not to be ignored

Act two, scene one, Geoff. From the top:
Enter Hostess, Fang and Snare

Oh, there! I thought we'd done that

Mutter of confusion in the ranks:
who's on, who's not

We have. Only Madam Quickly here forgot

I see. Of course. Let's get cracking then!

Thanks, Dudley. Thanks.

        ~

The stage is a rectangle
drawn on the worn board floor
in gaffer tape.

Never more a stage than when
empty like this:
a child's geometry of promise,
of unspoilt possibility.

Quickly, Fang and Snare, first on,
pause at its edge;
the rest straggle.

Sir Geoff/Sir John,
standing alone,
mouths lines towards the peeling ceiling.

Even offstage, he contrives
to upstage the rest –
attention-hogging sod!

Dudley calls for hush, twice,
and the company
falls silent.

Then a violent throat-clear from you-know-who
that echoes in this once-sacred place
like the cough of God.

        ～

Will 'a stand to 't?

Willa stand toot?

Will ah stand twit?

Ear and tongue in private conference
assay the options.

Cockney sparrer? EastEnders snarl and snide?
No to both. But then what's left
apart from the urbanoid Mummerset
that she's heard prattling from her own mouth
these past twenty minutes?

Why doesn't somebody help her?

Because it's phonetic free-for-all out there:
earls and princes with flagrant glottal stops,
the plummiest London bumpkins

Really, Shakespeare should have given Hal
a free hand with the wickeds and innits!

Will err stand tu-whit?

Within, she winces. But she'll get there yet.

 ∽

Enter –

the most thrilling word in all theatre,
as a teacher, a loving mentor, once said –

and they do:
Quickly and Fang a few steps ahead
of laggardly Snare.

Master Fang

Stop!

Dudley. Shooting one hand in the air
palm forward
like a traffic policeman –

traffic policeman!

Could we have that again, with a little more
agitation, please?
A little more

 ∽

flap and fluster?

He's said it. All but.

The swine! He wants me to do it like Margaret Rutherford

Do it like!

The one unforgivable crime! No insult bigger!

But I'm not Dame Margaret Rutherford, nor was meant

Even if my figure

Keeping her mouth shut,
she swings about
with an air of magnificent nonchalance
and following Snare and Fang
steps back, skips back, over the gaffer-tape line.

⁓

Bit of a tartar today –

Fang confides his sympathy
on a huff of Fisherman's Friend,
the lozenge knocking tinily against his back teeth –

I shouldn't let it get to you, pet.

She yields a smile
freighted with tears
destined to fall in their own sweet time.

Kind. But it always gets to you
don't you find?
in the end?

⁓

Even Fang's words
bless him for meaning well
feel like a trespass, an intrusion –

he's leaning too close for true comfort –
from the otherworld of blundering men.

She's surrounded by them right now –

Doll Tearsheet, there, the one exception,
and she looks like a boy:
trim and lissom as a foal
inside wrecked jeans and big loose lumberjack shirt,
hair cut short in a style designed to annoy
anybody over twenty-five.

But at least she's alive.
At least she's got some kick in her.

Good luck to you, Doll!

~

They're ready again at the gaffer-tape border.
Under starter's orders.
But Sir Geoff is having another of his whispers
with the director,
so they all have to wait:
other ranks, the expendable infantry, footlights fodder.

If you totted up the time spent just hanging around
how many hours
how many days

Hi diddledy dee
and it's nearly half-past three

~

Sir Geoff and Dudley appear to be in agreement –
Dudley nodding earnestly, Sir Geoff

flashing his gnashers –
when suddenly she sees it:

Sir John Falseteeth!

It's a revelation: the old fraud smiling
with a smile not his own
but some inane rictus
like a ventriloquist's dummy's
planted in the middle of his whiskers –
and he hasn't the least idea!

Fit climax to a career
along the well-signposted path
from Princelet, Ham of Denmark –
whose joke was that? –
via, yes! King Leer, then

what?

Prepostero!!!

to this windyguts here.

O unsatisfactory satire

O meagre consolation of the downtrodden
silently, cravenly, self-scathingly
railing at the victors

    ~

What's got into her, she wonders.
Ever since this morning,
when she left her not-quite husband –
Duff Lover III –
to his kitchen-table war zone

and one-man combat with the papers,
she's been scratching at an itch
that can't be reached.

Am I really such a

No, she won't use that word. It doesn't apply.
Give it to Dudley instead,
who's queening and policemanning for quiet again,
while sending yours truly a personal look
that's less Quickly, darling, than Off with her head!

Duly, the troops come to order,
take up their battle stations

and it's once more into the breach, dearies,
ours not to reason why.

       ~

Master Fang –

no hint of dotty headmistress or flustered hen here,
yet Dudley lets it pass: good omen –

have you entered the action?

It is entered.

Where's your yeoman? Is 't a lusty yeoman?

And she's away: her voice has found
accent, pitch, momentum
and she can ride it
jumping with ease the immediate hurdle:
Will he stand to it?

There! not so tricky.

And the three of them
canter at an even pace
through the opening exchanges, till
I am undone by his going –
when she picks up speed.

No point in belabouring or milking for their thin yield
Shakespeare's job-lot malapropisms –
indited to dinner to the Lubber's head in Lumbert Street –
but lend them the fury and dash they need
and the speech soars:

Yonder he comes, she roars,
and that arrant malmsey-nose knave Bardolph with him!

As Falstaff steps forward, it is apparent
he's not been expecting this; but Quickly has set the
    rhythm
and it's as much as he can do
to dance to it.

He dances like a bothered bear.

Away, varlets!

Fang and Snare retreat
but she, quickly, moves in, provocatively near,
and snatching Falstaff's bigshot command to Bardolph –

throw the quean in the channel! –

throws it back in his face.

I'm enjoying this:
thou honeysuckle villain! thou honey-seed rogue!

And these thous and wo'ts are just the thing –
Thou wo't, wo't thou? Thou wo't, wo't ta? –

for barking like a guard-dog
and summoning the law: the Lord Chief Justice, no less,
who comes running!

While she explains what's what,
arraigning her debtor
and laying the pathos on thick,
the false teeth hold their grim grin
but the rest of Falstaff
bloats and sags,
in a gut-sick confusion of awe and distress.

He'll never do it better!

What is the gross sum that I owe thee?
he manages.

Prompt for a final fearsome fleering:
recalling, with such a gush of detail
you can't but see the scene –
upon Wednesday in Wheeson week –
his biggest, his most appalling, betrayal:
thou didst swear to me then, as I was washing thy wound,
to marry me and make me my lady thy wife. Canst thou
    deny it?

Deny it if thou canst!

Just try it!

There's still a fund of cunning and whiskery cheek
in the old alpha male, but the Lord Chief Justice,
more than a match, browbeats him
till Sir John takes the plaintiff aside
for words that, because of business downstage,
the audience will not hear.

In this case:
Well played, my dear,
though I trust there won't be any more
of that sort of nonsense.

Then – Gower having delivered his news –
out loud:
As I am a gentleman!

To which she should reply:
Faith, you said so before –

only a catch in her throat
and a sudden ungovernable salt upwelling
bring proceedings to another
stumble and halt.

AIRS AND DITTIES OF NO MAN'S LAND

for Colin Matthews

CAPTAIN GIFFORD
SERGEANT SLACK

CAPT. There are two skeletons –

SGT. We are two skeletons –

BOTH two skeletons
hanging on wire in no man's land.

CAPT. Hanging on wire, you understand,
because no stretcher party can approach us.

SGT. Enemy fire.

CAPT. Hanging and silhouetted against the sky
like a pair of scarecrows,
ragged, mocked and tormented by the wind.

SGT. Crucified!

CAPT. That's blasphemy, sergeant.

SGT. With respect, sir, there was two thieves
hanging by our Saviour's side.

CAPT. I stand corrected.

SGT. You stand, I stand –

BOTH we both stand
unburied and unresurrected.
So, to pass the time, we let the wind
rummage in the hollows of our skulls
for memories and scraps of song and wisps of rhyme,
as follows.

CAPT.   Before divine creation,
the world was without form,
and void, the Bible tells us,
and so it is this evening
after the battle-storm.

Where shells fell, earth erupted
in fountains of black clay;
ancient trees somersaulted
and broke their backs; a landscape
jumped up and ran away.

How brave of two tired armies
to seek to nullify
our Maker's first-day handiwork,
obliterating geography
and cancelling the sky.

SGT. An old crow settled
on an observation tree
and looked through field-glasses
to see what he could see.

He saw rolling acres
of rubble and of mud,
sown with shells and bullets,
watered with men's blood.

He said, 'I'm no farmer
and maybe shouldn't talk,
but this new-fangled agriculture
ain't going to work.

'More to the purpose,
there's nothing for me to eat.'
At that, he relinquished
his uncomfortable seat,

and flapped off smartly
to the nest from whence he came.
And if I had a pair of wings,
I'd do the same.

CAPT. Snug in my dug-out, I hear Brother Rat bedding
down in his.

When we pass in the trench, I can barely smother
a disgusted shudder.

I know where he's dined and what he's dined on. I
know his mind.

Obscenely replete, he carries his corpulence on
fleet little feet.

And is it so fanciful to detect the sneer of the war
profiteer?

He owns this environment more than I do; he
likes living here.

He regards our inferno as his private club, where
he gets good grub – and lots of it.

Everything's plentiful! Everything's profit!

So, if I see him, I give him the widest possible
berth.

But when night falls and we've both gone to earth,
I feel differently.

We're both creatures who have burrowed deep to
snatch our brief sleep.

Like those cheery fellows in *The Wind in the
Willows*, we could be friends!

CAPT.   I'll tell you something, Sergeant Slack,
        I wish they'd told me long before:
        the tunes that march men off to war
        are not the same as march them back.

SGT.   You're quite right, sir. I for one
        never heard the band strike up
        for the benefit of some young pup
        being packed off home with both legs gone.

        They ought to write a few new marches
        in five-four time and clashing keys
        for chaps with shrapnel in their knees
        staggering out the gate on crutches.

        'A Blighty One', 'Stretcher Cases',
        and 'Toodle-oo' would be good titles
        for men with shrapnel in their vitals
        and missing limbs and blown-off faces.

        And for the blokes who've swallowed gas –

CAPT.   Thank you, sergeant, that's enough.
        Pipe down now and save your puff
        for the enemy's wind, percussion and brass.

SGT. Fritz is my friend:
when I lob a grenade
over the top,
he lobs one back –
it's a fair swap.

When a bullet bounces
off my tin hat,
I shoot at him,
obeying the law
of tit for tat.

As systems go,
it works pretty well.
No one's left short:
he gives me hell,
I give him hell.

Yes, I rub along fine
with my friend Fritz,
because we both know
that at the end,
when I've killed him
and he's killed me,
we'll be quits.

CAPT.	Someone takes up his mouth-organ and starts
	to breathe an old tune into it, or fingers out
	something almost forgotten on his penny whistle,
	or nudges his squeezebox for a sequence of chords
	that carries a melody that carries words
	that carry a meaning different for each of us,
	and the entire company stops to listen,
	as if listening, too, were a form of music,
	and our assembled silence, as big as an orchestra.

CAPT. I know a village some way away,
   where there's a little estaminet:
   the wine is filthy and the songs are flat,
   but the women are women, thank God for that!

BOTH The women are women, thank God for that!

CAPT. You drink your wine and you sing your song –

SGT. neither activity takes very long –

CAPT. then you climb the stairs to a room overhead –

SGT. and there's a woman, and there's a bed.

BOTH There's a woman, and there's a bed.

CAPT. You pay some money, but's it's not too much
   for the infinite heaven of a woman's touch.

SGT. It's infinite for a minute or two,
   then you're back downstairs with merci beaucoup.

BOTH Back downstairs with merci beaucoup.

CAPT. Another song and another glass of wine
   will send you merrily up the line –

SGT. where you spend all day and night in a trench –

CAPT. thinking of women –

SGT.   and practising your French.

BOTH Thinking of women and practising your French.

SGT. I was sharing a smoke
with the quarter-bloke,
when a lump of lead
took off most of his head.

I was having a chat
with some brass hat,
when a sniper's bullet
passed clean through his gullet.

The Padre and me
sat drinking tea,
when a five-nine shell
nobbled him as well.

Now, when I suggest cards,
my mates run yards
and I have to play patience –
all on acccount of those previous occasions
when I chanced to be near.
Do you call that fair?

CAPT. In my dream last night, two generals passed by,
neither appearing to be in a great hurry.
They stopped and looked down into the trench
   where I
and other men stood in a waist-deep slurry
of mud and sewage and stinking human rot.
The senior general said, 'Don't worry
about this insignificant little lot:
they're not being punished for something they did
   wrong;
they're just a company that HQ forgot
and have been festering in this pit so long,
to pull them out now would be too much bother.
Think of the bloody red tape! Think of the pong!
Best leave them be. I can show you some other,
much more interesting stuff. Come, follow me . . .'

SGT. I went to bed in a bath,
and the bath was dirty at that.
Now tell me, how stupid was that,
to go to bed in a bath
that was not just dirty but cold?
So I lay in the freezing mud,
till I woke up the colour of mud
and with a diabolical cold.

But never mind: tonight
I'll sleep in the open air,
under a blanket of air
that will keep me snug all night.
The wind will sing me to sleep
with its howling lullaby,
and in the sweet by-and-by
I'll either be dead or asleep.

And death is as good as a sleep,
don't you think?
Don't you think
death is as good as a sleep?

CAPT. They are drunken –

SGT.   but not with wine –

CAPT. they stagger –

SGT.   but not with strong drink –

BOTH the men who go over the top,
      the men who go over the brink.

SGT. They shout –

CAPT.   but not from high spirits –

SGT. they fall –

CAPT.   but not in a swoon –

BOTH the men who go into no man's land
      and won't be back soon.

A SALUTE TO THE MOONLIGHT

A Bit of a Tune

The moon's up early – *my* early;
    it's late for the moon.
And he's a full one, or nearly:
    crisp as a shop-bought macaroon.
Comforting, somehow, to see him so clearly.
    A benison and a boon.

With my toast and coffee out on the balcony,
    it's not too soon
to get some verbal euphony
    going, a bit of a tune
that will mark the 5:30 epiphany
    of bald and blotch-faced Mr Moon.

Nought-shaped, too rudimentary
    even to be a cartoon
character, he sits in a sky quite empty:
    no clouds strewn
haphazardly, no haze, just plenty
    of lovely absence. He's all aloooooooon . . .

Oh no, he's not. Even His Majesty
    is not immune
from interruption. Two nasty
    airliners have come to festoon
the dawn with their hasty
    graffiti, and then – blow me! – that buffoon

of the lower skyways, a huffy
    hot-air balloon,
bobs up and off *he*
    totters on his wind-willed horizontal swoon.
I take my toast and coffee
    indoors, and stay there till mid-afternoon.

The Conscripts

Shattered, the Monday morning darlings
set their proud
and pretty noses
towards work.

Weekend victims,
bombed
behind doll-perfect make-up,
their cigarette smoke tangling
with magnificent shampoos,
they muster
by misty bus-stops
at every edge of town.

Boyfriends and hurried breakfasts
behind them,
they are office fodder now,
brittle
but drilled
to a great, punctual purpose.

The tinny thrashing at their ears
speeds them
like a martial aphrodisiac;
their frank, unguarded yawns
are babyish
and leonine.

Espresso

Little cup of melancholy,
inch-deep well of the blackest
concentrate of brown,
it comes to your table without ceremony
and stands there shuddering
back to an inner repose.
Pinch it: it's still hot.

Soon, its mantle of bubbles
clears, but the eye –
all pupil, lustreless –
remains inscrutable.
Rightly so. This is your daily
communion with nothingness,
the nothingness within things.

Not to be sipped, it's a slug,
a jolt: one mouthful, then gone,
of comforting tarry harshness.
Which you carry now as a pledge
at the tongue's dead centre,
and the palate's, blessed
by both the swallowed moment
and its ghost, its stain.

Song of a Moment

You with your glass of electricity
    me with mine of mud
at a café table in our favourite city –
    and one of us said:

We're a perfect match, a reciprocity
    (if that's the right word) –
you with your glass of electricity
you with your eyes of startling audacity
    and me with mine of mud!

Truck

You've seen a truck –
        seen one you've seen thousands –
swagger purblind out
from the side of the road
and into mid-traffic
        without indicating

too daydreamy to notice
the swerving and hooting
        as it carves its passage
or just assuming you knew –
        somehow –
what it had been planning to do

the way a lover
will refrain from stating
        an urgent need –
desiring the effect
        without the tedium of its conveyance

and yet expect
every particle of the message
to be understood

Flute and Piano

'We're all in business by ourselves.'
– Bummidge, in Saul Bellow's *The Last Analysis*

All these people bulge into
the garden. If you contain the garden,
they bulge into that. The whole trio –
grandfather, mother and bulgy baby – are
argumentative for space
like planets. What they are is
tied to the ground like balloons. What they say
is tied to them like balloons.
                           Balloon
upon balloon in the afternoon!

The garden fills with floatings and
collisions. In agitated minor keys
a flute and piano play
the music of whales and businessmen.

Solar System

A pole's the South Pole,
a cherry-tree's the North,
and I am slung between them –

the planet's shut and dreaming eye
in my abstract hammock
of longitude and latitude –

not seeing but feeling
the far, fierce,
fatherly frown of the sun –

while an intermittent breeze
passes across my swaying,
on its way from somewhere to elsewhere.

Mother and Child

That's one jammy baby:
wrapped, plugged, trundled
in his very own buggy,
and wholly absorbed
in a dreamless, disasterless
sleep such as only
the newest of us enjoy.

As for the mother
of this oblivious boy:
frowning above him,
it's as if she belonged
to a different order of being
way beyond his seeing –
angel or puppeteer . . .

Now look how she lunges
into her task
of propelling him through the park!

Her bundle of steady breaths
and coddled heartbeats.

Prince of the immeasurable
shut-eye dark.

La Tartuga

for Bernard Turle

From one back window, piano practice:
repeated attacks on a trap of chords
repeatedly sprung;
    and, from another,
soprano arpeggios, intricate as hopscotch.

The dauntless human musical endeavour!

It's touch and go, too, in the animal kingdom,
where a tortoise tilts and bumps itself down
    some concrete steps,
like removal men managing
a large, odd,
    dusty, but once-loved
        item of farmhouse heirloom furniture,
while a bee gang carries out a spot raid
on the tight-squeeze flowers
of a shaken sage-bush.

From a Private Joke Book

Dr Demon

Fly of ill omen,
noisome blot,
he steered like a dodgem
round the room.

'Dr Demon,
I presume!'
I said, then dealt him
a lethal swat.

Now the newspaper
I happened to use
being all bespattered
with his jam, with his juice,

I had to bin it
that very minute.

The Ballad of P BINCE

'Who is that handsome rider?
    Is he the Prince?'
'No, my darling daughter,
    that is P BINCE.

'The Prince rides a horse,
    but P BINCE is cleverer –
marching to the wars
    on his high-stepping zebra.

'Lacking one leg,
    he must sit side-saddle
and gaze out sideways
    at the cheering rabble.

'With his hat in his hand
    and a snail shell on his head,
he trots across the land
    at no great speed.

'In fact, he's so slow,
    he may miss the slaughter
and live to marry you,
    my darling daughter.'

Academic

The moorhens, stooped and stalking
like Jacques Tati,
go nowhere near the automatic doors.

State of the Art

Alleluia! there it stood:
quintessence of coffee-table,
the unique, sleek, legendary item
in some near-extinct Brazilian wood,
black lacquer, brushed steel and sand-blasted plexiglass –

on which, of course, lay a big square book
shamelessly open at a double-page spread,
a seven-colour print job, celebrating
the very same table:
on which, unless my eyes deceived me –

Last of the Campus Poems

It's cosy in here, my seat
right next to the library window,
its panorama of snow, snow listlessly
adding itself
to already snow-daintified trees.

The computers stand idle,
inscrutable as barn owls,
and the muffled brouhaha the heating makes
makes for a very superior
brand of silence.

Term ends, and it's a poignant
satisfaction to know
that I have nothing new to say
on the subject of snow –
or, if I do have,
I am certainly not about to say it.

Evening

Astounding lights
that the murk and poison
the breath of London produce

water-ice pinks or greens
a tingling haze
at once grimy and luscious

festive tatters
of cirrus perhaps
snagged at the edge

shot bonfire orange
as the yolk of the sun
blops into the west

the whole production
rigged up
just to pique your eye for a minute

through smeared glass
as it might be
upstairs on the slow bus home

what to do with it all
except get out your paintbox
Mr James Mallord William Turner

and slap it down
as best you can
in the damnable absence of elbow room

Raga

A complete nervous system
is singing:
    supple, delirious
evening meditation music –

verandah shutters
wide open
to breezes and insects;
the horizon gulping the sun –

the bulbous, gravely jangled instrument
swooning
    ever more urgently
over a listening drone,

a drone that listens and responds to everything,

not least
the visceral throb,
the pulse and peristalsis
of two companionably babbling drums:

and the mind –
    scattered among the stars –
is content, at last,
with its place
    in the general scheme.

Chorus

O! for a Muse of fire that would ascend
beyond the spot where a bearded actor now stands
his voice a slightly fuzzy
baritone bellow

past the footlights
one of which is evidently
on the blink

over the stalls
releasing their expensive odours
brandy breaths and salacious
wafts of *Joy*

skirting the usual
gilt thingummybobs
cupids trumpets garlands eagles

up by the gods
where two late arrivals
shuffle like gannets
for a perch on the perilous cliff-ledge

out through the roof and into the night sky

which has not yet ceased to offload
its surplus grief
on the traffic of bleary black cabs and thrumming
    umbrellas

A Pub Band

'Behold the world, how it is whirled round,
And for it is so whirl'd, is named so.'
– Sir John Davies: *Orchestra*

From where we stand
this spinning ball
our mother earth
it's all dark backward
and abysm
so to speak
so far as birth

The moon her bleak
sister or daughter
we're told sprang
from some minor casual
cataclysm
a bump in the night
a bit of a fright

So far so bad
and in the light
the light of the dark
backward etcetera
isn't it enough
that nub of the night sky
to be getting on with

No not enough
we need to know
not just the dry
fact of the moon
but a better myth
a more outlandish truth
to help explain us

Numbers numb us
tell us nothing
we can feel
the clock's not real
always a tick
away from midnight
an empty trick

Better rather
join the spacious
dance of the planets
igneous gaseous
far out or farther
these carbuncles
our aunts and uncles

And their father
or mother sun
from whom they were spun
and other suns
that splash the dark
inviting assent
from our infinitesimal spark

Rabbits and Concrete

Rabbits, too many to count,
were out in the moonlight.

They had come to inspect
the world of men,
or, in the absence of men,
the world of concrete and moonlight.

And the wink of their tails
as they scaddled about
was like a salute to the moonlight.

Neddy and the Night Noises

Neddy Bumwhistle jolts awake in the dark.
Insomnia's big comic-strip exclamation mark
twitches like defective neon above his head.
At least he's in the familiar slum of his own bed:
no body beside him; nobody, perhaps, for miles around . . .
But hang about, what's that weird, squeaky-bedspring
    sound?
He's heard it before. Don't tell him. Ah, yes –
it's the dawn chorus (so-called), that murk, that mess
of repetitive, uppity fanfare and squabbling fuss
by which the birds of the city announce, 'Hi, it's us!
Three in the morning! Rise and shine!' The din
swells, as several car alarms join in,
some cats either start a fight or engage in sex
(hard to tell which), and the whole complex
fugue of the small hours – over a bass line of A-road
    rumble –
gets into full swing. Neddy's own mumble
of shock and disgust is a mere grace-note;
the same, when he dislodges a plug of catarrh from his
    throat.
There's no noise he can make that will not be in tune
with this all-embracing symphony, composed by the man
    in the moon.
He tries a fart, a tad louder than intended,
and it's answered at once by an ambulance siren and
    thereby blended
into the general texture. The music of the spheres
(which everybody has heard of, but nobody hears)
must, thinks poetic Neddy, sound like this.
Sod it! Grunting, he grapples out of bed in search of a piss,

sharply needed after the previous evening's nine
(or was it ten?) pints. Minutes later, bladder's fine,
but brain's still rattling like a high-street charity extortion
    box.
Sleep's off the agenda now. On with socks
and knitted muffler. Time for a brew-up and toast.
The flame on the gas-ring jump-flutters as if it has seen a
    ghost,
but soon everything's steaming and singeing sweetly
in the dug-out, the nightwatchman's cabin, the none-too-
    neatly
ordered alchemist's den of Neddy's kitchen.
Thank God for such simple comforts, when life's a bitch in
so many ways (too many to count right now)!
Stir the sludge in your mug, Neddy, unfrazzle yon brow,
and let the night out there with its meaningless clatter
barrel past unheeded. Nothing can matter
to a man with a mouthful of perfectly charred
sliced white chomping in his head. Nothing's too hard
for the soul that's sluiced with slurps of strong, sugary tea.
Unless . . . What luck (and does anyone suffer worse luck
    than he?)
that his idle eye should at that moment light
on the very thing from which his conscious mind has been
    in flight
since yesterday morning, when, in a rage
ignited by the reading (and rereading) of a certain page
in a certain magazine, he flung it across the room
with a spattering of curses to lend it speed. A sour gloom
curdled his spirits the rest of the day:
from lunchtime breakfast at the reeking café
along the road, through an ugly ten minutes on the phone
to his live-out (now ex-) lover, Jan, back home alone

(and twice as bothered) for an hour or two,
then out again to the educational zoo
where he runs the weekly poetry workshop (rude
to everyone in turn), all the way to getting grimly slewed
in some of the more blighted pubs in town.
Bed caught him, by a miracle, as he spiralled down, down,
    down . . .
But sleep offered only the briefest reprieve from feeling.
Now as rawly awake as the bare bulb hanging from the
    ceiling,
Neddy in his kitchen must return to consider the problem
of why the *Poetry Gazette* has set out to nobble him.
Picking the rag up from where it crash-landed
on a scree of beer cans and pizza boxes, he scans it
and in seconds is finger-tapping his own name,
next to a three-figure number. Oh, the shame!
Scandal, more like it – passing off as a 'survey'
a piece of the most malign, craven, deceitful, scurvy
reputation-rigging he has ever seen.
A poetry popularity poll? I mean!
And himself (allegedly) at two hundred and ninety-six?
Do me a favour! Less popular than all these hicks?
He strums his finger close to the very top.
Then closer. Closer still. Then he has to stop,
or enter the negative space of the minus numbers –
and he's not yet ready to play the Christopher Columbus
of black-hole exploration. Top is fine, thanks.
Divinely appointed to the highest ranks,
however, and the Muse's most trusted amanuensis,
he knows to his personal cost that eminence is
no doddle. With T for talent scored on his forehead,
back-cover mugshots show him perpetually worried,
as well he might be, given the grave risks and paltry rewards

that the life of a beer-fuelled Baudelaire affords.
Envied and hated by the gang of charlatans and hacks
who use the reviews to scratch each other's backs
but couldn't tell genuine genius if it grabbed them by the
    nuts,
he's taken more than his share of snubs, cuts,
sneers, maulings and impudent condescension
from them, while never once catching the attention
of the dolts and dodos who dosh out the big money.
Five slim and widely slighted volumes wiser, the funny
thing is he hasn't packed the whole caper in. What keeps
him going, in a world so rotten it's strictly the creeps
who collect the cash and cachet (crumpet, as well,
he's started to notice)? Some nook of Dante's Hell
waits toasty-warm for them, no doubt, but meanwhile
for the unknown hero it's a case of 'Smile, boys, that's the
    style!'
Ever thus . . . Neddy lets his *Poetry Gazette*
flop to the floor. Flashing teeth, he'll show them yet.
One last swig, and he rests his mug with an untidy clunk
and teaspoon jitter. The clock on the wall bites chunk
    after chunk
off time. His fridge hums its simple song.
A rat on a top-secret errand skitters along
the trench behind the skirting-board. Pipes gurgle. Neddy
burps antiphonally. A new, heady
sense of purpose grips him and, by chance, pencil and
    paper stand ready.